THE COLOURS OF ANOTHER AGE

THE ROTHSCHILD AUTOCHROMES 1908–1912

Edited by Victor Gray
with contributions by Colin Harding, Sophieke Piebenga
and Lionel de Rothschild

THE ROTHSCHILD ARCHIVE

The Rothschild Archive gratefully acknowledges
the support and assistance of Waddesdon Manor
(The Rothschild Collection), National Trust,
and the National Media Museum, Bradford.

Published in 2007 by
The Rothschild Archive
New Court
St. Swithin's Lane
London EC4P 4DU

© Victor Gray, Colin Harding, Sophieke Piebenga

Designed by Sally McIntosh
Printed by Beacon Press
Francis Atterbury

A catalogue record for this book is available from
the British Library
ISBN-13 9780953847631
ISBN 0953847632

CONTENTS

A hugely atmospheric image
of a Japanese tea-house in
an unidentified garden
(see Nos. 23 and 24).

INTRODUCTION

My grandfather and namesake, Lionel de Rothschild, was a perfectionist. Not only did he demand and expect the very highest standards but applied those same exacting standards to himself: in the twenty short years between the wars he created at Exbury one of the largest and finest woodland gardens in the world, largely devoted to rhododendrons and azaleas, containing species collected from the wild and hybrids he had made himself. One of his contemporaries remarked on his discerning eye for colour and his mastery of the art of anticipation: he could feel by instinct the effect of his designs. This book shows those same qualities at work in an earlier passion, photography; the same feel for colour and light that he brought to planning his garden is exhibited in these Autochromes. It is interesting that while he showed the same skills in both, these two arts lie at opposite ends of the spectrum in relation to time – the photograph a matter of seconds, the garden a matter of years. Lionel was justly proud of his photography and in addition to the glass plates that survive we have two huge albums with his best black and white prints showing the same virtuosity in composition. His Autochromes give a glimpse of a vanished world, a world redolent of Edwardian insouciance, seen for once not in jerky cinefilm or grainy black and white but in luminous colour and it is that, I think, that adds to our poignant sense, in Larkin's words, of 'never such innocence again'.

Lionel de Rothschild

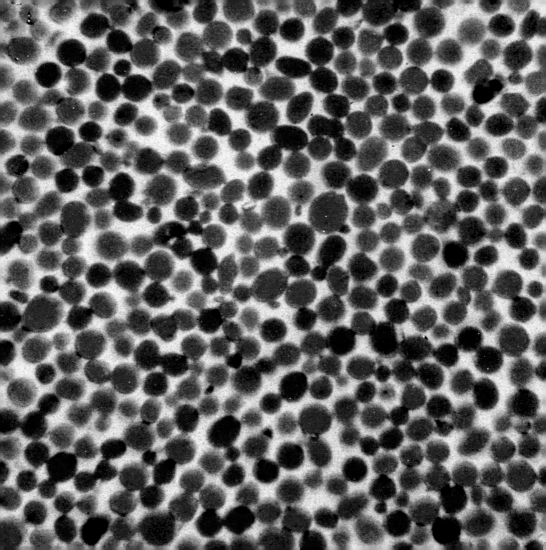

Autochromes: *the dawn of colour photography*

COLIN HARDING

The quest for colour

In 1839, when photographs were seen for the first time, they were regarded with a sense of wonder. However, amazement was soon tempered by disappointment. How could a process that captured the forms of nature with exquisite detail fail so dismally to record its colours? The search for a practical process of colour photography soon became photography's 'Holy Grail'. Yet, while scientists, businessmen and experimenters grappled with the problem, the public became impatient. Photographers, eager to satisfy their customers, took the matter into their own hands – literally – and began to add colour to their monochrome images. In the right, skilled, hands, effects of great subtlety and beauty could be achieved. Even at its very best, however, hand-colouring remained an arbitrary and ultimately unsatisfactory solution. What was desired was a purely photographic process that would transform photography from being, in W.H.F. Talbot's famous phrase, 'The Pencil of Nature' to 'The Paintbrush of Nature'.

However, before colour could be faithfully reproduced, the nature of light had first to be clearly understood. The scientific investigation of light and colour had begun in the 17th century when Sir Isaac Newton famously split sunlight using a prism to show that it was actually a combination of the seven colours of the spectrum. Nearly 200 years later, in 1861, James Clerk Maxwell conducted an experiment to prove that all colours can be reproduced through

Enlargement of an Autochrome plate showing the distribution of dyed potato starch granules.

mixing red, green and blue light. Maxwell made three separate magic lantern-slides of a piece of tartan ribbon, through red, green and blue filters. These slides were then projected through the same filters using three separate magic lanterns. When the three images were carefully superimposed, they combined to produce a single coloured image which was a recognisable reproduction of the original subject. Known as additive colour synthesis, this principle was to form the basis of the Autochrome process.

If the fundamental theory was now understood, a practical method of colour photography remained elusive. Several pioneers did succeed in making colour photographs but their processes were complex, impractical and not commercially viable. Despite its theoretical importance, their work was to be of limited practical value because the photographic emulsions of the time were limited in their colour sensitivity. It was not until the end of the nineteenth century that the first so-called 'panchromatic' plates, sensitive to all colours, were produced. Now, at last, the way lay clear for the invention of the first practicable method of colour photography – the Autochrome process, invented in France by Auguste and Louis Lumière.

The birth of the Autochrome

The Lumière brothers are best known as film pioneers with their invention of the *cinématographe* in 1895, but they had also been experimenting with colour photography for several years. In 1904, they presented their results to the French Académie des Sciences. Three years later they had perfected their process and begun the commercial manufacture of *Autochrome* plates. On 10 June 1907, the first public demonstration of their process took place at the offices of the French newspaper *L'Illustration*. The event was a triumph. News of the discovery spread quickly and critical response was rapturous. Upon seeing his first Autochrome, the eminent photographer, Alfred Stieglitz could scarcely contain his enthusiasm: 'The possibilities of the process seem to be unlimited ... soon the world will be color-mad, and Lumière will be responsible.'[1]

The manufacture of Autochrome plates, undertaken at the Lumière factory in Lyon, was a complex industrial process. First, transparent starch grains were passed through a series of sieves to isolate grains between ten and fifteen microns (thousandths of a millimetre) in diameter. Many different types of starch were tried, but the humble potato was found to give the best results. These microscopic starch grains were separated into batches, dyed red, green and violet, mixed together and spread over a glass plate coated with a sticky varnish. Next, carbon black (charcoal powder) was spread over the plate

(above)
The Lumière brothers.

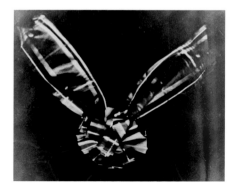

(left)
Maxwell's ribbon, 1861, a key experiment in the history of colour photography.

to fill in any gaps between the coloured starch grains. A roller submitted the plate to a pressure of five tons per square centimetre in order to spread the grains and flatten them out. On every square inch of the surface of an Autochrome plate there are about four million transparent starch grains, each one of which acts as a tiny coloured filter. Finally, the plate was coated with a panchromatic photographic emulsion.

Although complicated to make, Autochrome plates were comparatively simple to use – a fact that greatly enhanced their appeal to amateur photographers. Moreover, they did not require any special apparatus. Photographers could use their existing cameras. However, they did have to remember to place the Autochrome plate in the camera with the plain glass side nearest the lens so that light passed through the filter screen before reaching the sensitive emulsion. Exposures were made through a yellow filter which corrected the excessive blue sensitivity of the emulsion and gave a more accurate colour rendering. This, combined with the light-filtering effect of the dyed starch grains, meant that exposure times were very long – about thirty times that of monochrome plates. A summer landscape taken in the midday sun still required at least a one second exposure. In cloudy weather, this could be increased to as much as ten seconds or more. Spontaneous 'snapshot' photography was out of the question and the use of a tripod was essential.

Following exposure, the plate underwent development to produce a positive transparency. In the finished plate, transmitted light, passing through the millions of tiny red, green and violet transparent starch grains, combines to give a full colour image.

No mere technical description, however, can adequately convey the inherent luminous beauty and dream-like quality of an Autochrome, reminiscent of Pointillist or Impressionist painting. This beauty has a very down-to-earth explanation. In theory, the coloured starch grains were distributed randomly. In practice, however, some grouping of grains of the same colour is inevitable. Whilst individual starch grains are invisible to the naked eye, these clumps are visible – the reason for the Autochrome's unique and distinctive beauty.

Following highly favourable publicity in the summer of 1907, photographers were naturally keen to try out Autochrome plates for themselves. At first, there was frustration: demand far outstripped supply. It was not until October that the first, eagerly awaited consignment of plates went on sale in Britain. By 1913, the Lumière factory was making 6,000 Autochrome plates a day, in a range of different sizes.

Success qualified

The complexity of the manufacturing process meant that Autochrome plates were inevitably more expensive than monochrome. To compensate for this, Autochrome plates were sold in boxes of four, rather than the usual twelve. In 1910, a box of four quarter-plates cost three shillings (15p), compared with two shillings (10p) for a dozen monochrome plates. Their relatively high cost was the subject of frequent comment in the photographic press. Whilst of relatively little concern, of course, to wealthy amateurs such as Lionel de Rothschild, this clearly did have some effect in limiting the process's wider popularity.

In its annual survey for 1908, *Photograms of the Year* commented on the growing interest in the Autochrome process. The *Salon* Exhibition of 1908, for example, contained almost 100 Autochromes by leading figures such as Edward Steichen, Baron Adolf de Meyer, Alvin Langdon Coburn and James Craig Annan. These were the subject of considerable critical attention. However, after a brief period of intense interest, most 'artistic' photographers abandoned the process. There are a number of reasons for this. First Autochromes were extremely difficult to exhibit. For private viewing they could, of course, simply be held up to the light. However, for ease and comfort, Autochromes were usually viewed using special stands, called diascopes, which incorporated a mirror. These gave a brighter image and allowed several people to look at the plate at the same time. For public exhibition, Autochromes were also projected using a magic lantern. Stereoscopic Autochromes, viewed in stereoscopes, were particularly effective:

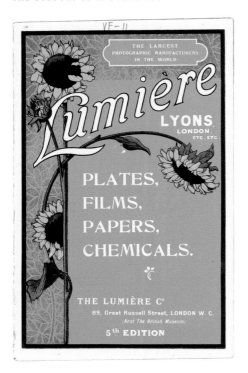

The cover of the Lumière Co, London, catalogue, published in about 1912 when they described themselves proudly as 'The Largest Photographic Manufacturers in the World'.

as *The Photographic News* noted in 1908: '... when the effect of relief is joined to a life-like presentation in colour the effect is quite startling in its reality. It is not easy to imagine what the effect of anything of this kind would have been on our ancestors ... Witchcraft would have been but a feeble, almost complimentary term, for anything so realistic and startling.'[2] Many photographers were bewitched by the twin spells of depth and colour, including Lionel de Rothschild who owned a couple of stereo cameras and took many stereo Autochromes.

Another, possibly more significant reason for the Autochrome's loss of popularity amongst some photographers was the fact that the process did not allow for any manipulation of the final image. For many photographers, the Autochrome, unlike printing processes such as gum and bromoil, was a totally unresponsive and therefore ultimately unsatisfactory medium, inherently unsuited to the 'pictorialist' aesthetic. As the name itself suggests, the beauty of the Autochrome depended largely on the process itself rather than on any personal intervention by the photographer, whose role was confined to composition rather than manipulation.

Crucially, for the first time, photographers now had to develop an empathy with colour closer to that of painters. As the distinguished photographer Robert Demachy soon realised: '... the Lumière process will make us learn the intricate laws of colour. It will not be done in a day, and we must resign ourselves to the inevitable atrocities that the over-confident amateur is going to thrust upon us.'[3] However, it was by no means just 'over-confident amateurs' that were prone to produce 'atrocities'. Many prominent photographers found themselves adrift in an alien world of colour – a world that they were very glad to leave behind as soon as the initial novelty and excitement had worn off.

The Autochromist at large

The vast majority of Autochromes were taken by amateur photographers, attracted to the process by the novelty of colour combined with its comparative simplicity. In 1908, R. Child Bayley, editor of *Photography* magazine, wrote an article on the process for *The Strand* magazine. Bayley was keen, above all, to stress its advantages for the amateur photographer: 'There is now a process by which we can get a faithful picture in the camera, giving us the colours of Nature in a most startlingly truthful way. Moreover, it is essentially an amateur process. It calls for no great amount of skill and takes no great time to work.'[4] Many amateur photographers, including, of course, Lionel de Rothschild, eagerly embraced the world of colour that was now, finally, within their grasp. Possessing, as he did, money, time, skill and motivation, it would indeed have been surprising had he not decided to become an enthusiastic user of Autochrome plates.

The subjects chosen by this first generation of colour photographers reflected both the possibilities of the Autochrome process and its inherent technical limitations. A colourful subject was paramount and, even if absent in nature, could always be introduced through props such as parasols. Portraiture was, of course, a very popular application. Whilst indoor portraiture was possible, the long exposure times required meant that most portraits were taken outdoors. The sunny garden portrait with a background of a flower border or trellis quickly became a visual *cliché* of the Autochrome process. Gardens themselves, with or without people, were also a popular subject. As *The British Journal of Photography* noted: 'Colour is the very essence of the delight of the garden ... The garden lover wants photographs as records of what he has accomplished, and which will last long after the glory of the original has departed.'[5] Flowers were probably the most frequent subject, since they possessed the essential twin attributes of colour and immobility. Photography's potential as a means of documenting 'reality' had, of course, long been realised but the Autochrome process brought a whole new dimension to the pursuit of realism – the recording of colour as well as form. The value of the process for scientific, medical and documentary photography was recognised almost immediately and Autochrome plates were widely used to photograph botanical and natural history specimens.

Photography shapes our vision of the world and travel is one of the greatest motives for taking photographs. The ability to capture the world in colour was one of the major reasons for the popularity of the Autochrome. Undoubtedly the most extraordinary example of its use was the project initiated by the wealthy French banker Albert Kahn. In 1909, Kahn decided to create his *Archives de la Planète* – 'a photographic inventory of the surface of the planet as it is occupied, and managed, by man at the beginning of this twentieth century'. Kahn employed a team of photographers who were dispatched all over the world. The result, spanning over twenty years, was a collection of 72,000 Autochromes taken in 38 different countries. Whilst on an entirely different scale, of course, many wealthy amateur photographers followed Kahn's example and used the Autochrome process to record their travels all over the world. Lionel de Rothschild was, in many ways, typical when he used it to photograph scenes in the Mediterranean and North Africa.

The success of Autochrome plates prompted the appearance of several other additive colour processes, all based on the principle of a screen made up of microscopic colour filters. None of them, however, was as commercially successful and most are now long forgotten. Despite limitations, the Autochrome process dominated the market for colour photography for nearly 30 years. In 1932, responding to a growing trend away from the use of glass plates towards roll film, the Lumières introduced a version of their process which used sheet film as the emulsion support. Marketed under the name 'Filmcolor', within a couple of years this had virtually replaced glass Autochrome plates. However, these changes occurred at precisely the same time that other manufacturers were successfully developing new multi-layer colour films which reproduced colour through subtractive synthesis – thus doing away with the need for filter screens. It was with these pioneering multi-layer films such as Kodachrome that the future of colour photography lay. The Autochrome was confined to history but it retains its place as not only the first colour process but also probably the most beautiful photographic process ever invented.

Colin Harding is Curator of Photographic Technology, the National Media Museum, Bradford

---

NOTES

1   Alfred Stieglitz, 'The Color Problem for Practical Work Solved', *Photography*, 13 August, 1907, p 136.
2   *The Photographic News*, 6 March, 1908, p 234.
3   Robert Demachy, 'The Pictorial Side in France', *Photograms of the Year*, 1908, p 62.
4   R. Child Bayley, 'The New Colour Photography', *The Strand* magazine, April 1908, pp 412-4.
5   *The British Journal of Photography*, Colour Supplement, 7 July, 1922, p28.

FURTHER READING

Brian Coe, *Colour Photography: The First Hundred Years* (London: Ash & Grant, 1978).
Jack H. Coote, *The Illustrated History of Colour Photography* (Surbiton: Fountain Press Ltd, 1993).
Pamela Roberts, *A Century of Colour Photography* (London: Carlton Books, 2007).
John Wood, *The Art of the Autochrome: The Birth of Colour Photography* (Iowa City: University of Iowa Press, 1993).

LIONEL DE ROTHSCHILD, *Autochromist*

VICTOR GRAY

A life at full speed

Lionel Nathan de Rothschild could not have denied that fortune had smiled on him. He was born on 25 January 1882, the son of Leopold de Rothschild, one of the three partner-brothers in the family banking business of N.M. Rothschild & Sons founded three quarters of a century before by Lionel's great-grandfather. It was now at the height of its fortunes, one of the most powerful international financial forces of the age.

In a real sense, his course was set for him from birth. He served his years at Harrow before going up to Trinity College Cambridge where his father had preceded him. On leaving, the family business beckoned respectfully but compellingly and to New Court, the bank's offices in the City, he duly went at the age of 21.

He stayed there for the rest of his life. New Court would provide the position and income that would fuel Lionel's life but (as yet) it was no strait-jacket. Life offered a myriad of opportunities to the wealthy Edwardian. Lionel, in his twenties, pursued them with vigour, a young man of fortune let loose on the world. Early in September 1903 he was fined £5 for driving a motor-car at an excessive speed (22.5 m.p.h.) on the Great North Road. Lionel had discovered the attractions of speed. In 1905, he had a fine new Siddeley-Wolseley specially built for him with a view to entering it for the Gordon Bennett international endurance competition. Only

---

Lionel Nathan de Rothschild, 1882-1942.

his father's intervention prevented him from driving it in the Isle of Man trials – perhaps wisely since car and driver ended up embedded in a shop window. His passion for driving was undaunted. In October 1905 he accepted an impromptu challenge from his French cousin, Henri de Rothschild, to race from Paris to Monte Carlo in their respective 60 h.p. Mercedes. Lionel won, completing the 600 mile journey in 18 hours.

In 1905 he found a new way of exploring this passion for speed. Two years before, Sir Alfred Harmsworth, proprietor of the *Daily Mail*, had funded the world's first power-boat racing trophy, The Harmsworth Trophy. Lionel bought one of the new Napier motor-boats and fitted it with the largest six-cylinder engine yet built. Sharing the crewing with his friend, the Hon. John Scott-Montagu, he entered the 1905 Challenge in the Bay of Arcachon in France, raced over 35 miles. They crossed the finishing-line in a winning time of 2 hours, 2 minutes, 26 seconds. In the following year, again with Scott-Montagu, he beat the world water-speed record at 28.8 knots and in 1907 went on to win the prestigious Perla del Mediterraneo.

The excitement of travel had also come into the picture. In 1905 Lionel set off with his driver and mechanic, Martin Harper, on a trip to Rome in a 40 h.p. Mercedes. It was to be the first of many trips – and many cars. The following year, he was hurtling through Italy at 40m.p.h. with Lady Helen Vincent, Muriel Wilson and Winston Churchill and was recording in the magazine, *The Car*, a motoring expedition to Algeria. In time these trips across Europe and beyond would provide many of the opportunities for Lionel's photographic forays.

Behind the lens

When Lionel took to the camera is not clear. In his late teens, he was already photographing gardens in Italy. His 1906 article in *The Car* is illustrated with his own photographs. In the spring of 1909, Lionel's driver was recording a delay on their journey around Spain while his employer spent two days photographing the cathedral in Burgos.

The arrival in Britain in 1907 of the Auto-chrome, the first commercially viable colour photographic process, invented in France by the Lumière brothers, created a sensation among photographers, and particularly among those wealthy enough to afford the considerable cost of the photographic plates needed for the process. Lionel, always keen to be in the van-guard, was quick to experiment with colour. His earliest Autochromes appear to date from 1908 and by 1909 he was bringing back from his tour of Spain colour plates of Granada and other points *en route*.

Lionel (left) at the wheel of one of his many cars.

Throughout the following year, Lionel took many Autochrome plates as well as con-tinuing to shoot in black and white. The garden remained a favourite subject. In England, the gardens of the family houses at Ascott in Buckinghamshire and Gunnersbury in west London were photographed time and again, while in France his cousin Edmond invited him to his home at Boulogne-sur-Seine outside Paris, where he photographed both the formal gardens and the Japanese Garden. It seems highly probable that on one of these visits he would have met Edmond's neighbour, Albert Kahn, another Jewish banker excited by the Autochrome, an interest which was to lead on to his hugely ambitious project, *Les Archives de la Planète*. The conversation must have turned upon the potential of the Autochrome.

The most enthusiastic phase of Lionel's interest dates from the short period from 1908 to 1912, culminating in a long series of photographs taken on his honeymoon. In March 1907, Lionel's distant French cousin Robert had married Gabrielle Nelly Régine Beer, the daughter of a French banker. Lionel may well have attended the marriage in Paris. Certainly at some stage, either now or in the next couple of years, he met and grew close to Nelly's younger sister Marie-Louise Eugénie (known affectionately as Mariloo). On 8 October 1912 Lionel de Rothschild M.P. married the twenty-year old Mariloo in Paris. Their four-week honeymoon was spent in Italy, visiting Rome and the area around Naples. Together with his new wife, Lionel had brought along his camera and Autochrome plates. Mariloo's patience must have been sorely tried as Lionel composed and shot view after view.

Life closes in

The honeymoon proved to be something of a photographic watershed. After 1912, the photographs continue, but in diminishing numbers. Perhaps it was marriage that changed Lionel's pattern of life, or the growth of his political life (he had been M.P. for Mid-Bucks since 1910), or the responsibilities of the Bank, where the increasing debility of the older generation of senior partners must have been throwing new burdens on Lionel and his two brothers. Whatever the reasons, he seems to have shown less interest in the Autochrome after this time. And so it was that Lionel's most active phase as a photographer coincides almost exactly with the birth and rise of the Autochrome itself, which hit England in 1907 and was already beginning to lose its edge for the popular photographer by the time war broke out in 1914.

The onset of war was to change Lionel's life dramatically. The family bank was in the hands of three ageing brothers, the senior of whom, Natty, Lord Rothschild, now 75, was increasingly handicapped by deafness. Lionel had been a 2nd Lieutenant in the Royal Bucks Hussars since 1903, but with the outbreak of war it was felt more important that he stay to assist in the affairs of the bank. He served in the Reserves as a Major in the Buckinghamshire Yeomanry and quickly accepted the position of Vice-Chairman of the Central Jewish Recruiting Committee when it was set up in 1915, making available offices in New Court. He also managed the City of London's recruiting office, eventually earning an OBE for his war work.

By the end of the war, all of the older generation at New Court were dead, as was Lionel's brother, Evelyn, killed in action in Palestine in 1917. Lionel and his surviving brother, Anthony, found themselves, in their thirties, at the head of one of the most widely known firms in international banking. Lionel now also found himself in possession of two family estates, neither of them ideal for a young family (there were now two children and two more would follow). By 1919, he had taken the decision to make his future in Hampshire. He bought Exbury House, near to Inchmery House, the property on the Solent which he had acquired at the time of his marriage. He extended the house and then turned to the gardens. It was on this soil that Lionel would explore to the full his most lasting passion in the shape of horticulture, eventually developing a superb new garden where he could pursue his love of rhododendrons. In later years, he would come to joke that he was 'a gardener by profession and a banker by hobby' and his work as a collector and hybridiser of rhododendrons would earn him an international reputation.

Little wonder if Lionel's other interests waned. He continued in the post-war years to take photographs, now only in black and white and mainly on family holidays. Increasingly they took on the form of 'photographs of record', pasted into albums with (welcome) annotations. Rarely did they show the careful composition and concern for light and texture of the earlier images.

Lionel died of cancer in 1942 at the age of sixty. The inter-war years had been difficult ones for a banker and Lionel and Anthony, as leading members of the Jewish community in England, had been all too aware of the extent of Nazi persecution of the Jews in mainland Europe. They had worked tirelessly to help Jewish refugees. The carefree days of motoring and speedboat racing, of Edwardian society gatherings and explorations in Europe and Africa must have seemed a world away. Somewhere in a cupboard at Exbury, however, that world remained locked away, captured in colour and printed on glass, awaiting the moment when, held up to a different light in a different age, they would spring once more into life, reawakening in their soft and surprising colours the freshness of a world long lost.

A world rediscovered

The photographic gene in Lionel de Rothschild was handed on to his descendants. Edmund, his eldest son, was a keen cine-photographer in the middle years of the century, his eldest grandson Nicholas would become a film-maker in his own right and Nick's brother, Lionel, a highly proficient photographer, sharing his grandfather's particular passion for garden photographs.

The only picture of Lionel as photographer, taken by his wife at Salisbury Army Camp, May 1914.

A striking black and white image from Lionel's trip to Egypt, 1910.

It was the younger Lionel who first recognised the significance of the piles of glass plates which had lain hidden in a cupboard beneath a window at Exbury, probably since the house had been first occupied by Lionel and Mariloo. Dusty and uncared for, a few had been cracked and the emulsion was peeling from others. But for most of them, it took only the effort to hold them up to the light to understand the enduring beauty of what had been captured more than eighty years before.

What was not clear at that stage was the rarity of what had survived, protected by its neglected hiding-place. The fashion for Autochrome photography, which began with a desperate rush in 1907, matured, in only a few years, into a more measured recognition of both the qualities and the drawbacks of the process. A few committed Autochromists carried on into the 1920s and beyond. Most amateurs soon resorted to the ease and economy of black-and-white.

In its country of origin, collections of Autochromes had been longer and more carefully cherished, inspired in part by the high peak of the magnificent collection of Albert Kahn, with its 72,000 Autochromes. Some 600 of an estimated 800 Autochromes taken by Jean-Baptiste Tournassoud, as official photographer attached to the French army, survive among the collections of the *Etablissement de Communication et de Production Audiovisuelle de la Défense*. In America, the collections of the *National Geographic* magazine, which published more than a thousand Autochromes between 1914 and 1937, remain intact, while the work of one late-flowering amateur Autochromist, Frank Lauder, shooting 1,200 images of and around his native Kansas City in the early 1930s, remains in the City Library. Other collections survive around the world in places as widely scattered as Warsaw and British Columbia, Helsinki and Stuttgart.

In Britain, collections of Autochromes are rare. The National Media Museum in Bradford has some 2,000 plates, both from its own collections and from the absorbed collections of the Royal Photographic Society. They embrace the work of many photographers, the largest collection among them by a British photographer being that of John Cimon Warburg. Outside Bradford, the largest collection by a single photographer in a public collection appears to be not that of a British but a Russian Autochromist, the novelist Leonid Andreyev, whose 80 plates, along with black-and-white photographs, were gifted to the University of Leeds Russian Archive by his descendants.

It became clear, therefore, that this collection by Lionel de Rothschild, hidden away for so long, was by far the largest representation of the work of a single Autochromist to have survived in Britain (though it may well be that the centenary will bring others to light). It would have astonished Lionel – banker, horticulturalist, motorist, philanthropist – to find himself recalled now as a significant photographer. His work reflects the interests of a keen amateur, but, time and again, in looking at the images, one is forced to recognise the work of someone who had a fine eye for composition, for the juxtaposition of light and shade and the interplay of colour. In his colour work, as in his black-and-white photography, he showed a patient, even pain-staking approach to what he was doing. The results rise far above the amateur or the average.

The Rothschild Autochrome Collection

The cameras on which Lionel took many of these images happily survive and form part of the collection now in The Rothschild Archive. The magnificent half-plate tropical reflex camera, manufactured by Marion & Co. Ltd. of London still gleams at you as it slides smoothly from its leather case, stamped with the owner's name and address. Lacquered-brass screws and fittings are embedded in a polished teak body with a brass plate bearing the initials 'L de R', and as you open its various panels, a red leather viewing hood and bellows emerge. More modest is the compact Newman and Guardia stereoscopic Sibyl camera, on which Lionel shot almost 150 stereo images to be gazed at through a hand-held viewer, revealing the twin marvels of coloured and three-dimensional images, combined together as never before – as real as it could get in 1912. These, together with the dark-slides and plates and the yellow filters through which Autochromes were shot, would have accompanied Lionel in the back of his motor-car, along bone-shaking roads, across the Alps, on ferries and into the desert of North Africa.

Of the 734 surviving plates, just under ninety are portraits of friends and family. They are among the most compelling of the images, some subjects staring direct into the lens with the practised familiarity of a social group comfortable with the camera, others posed at ease, usually in a garden setting where the light was reliable and the setting easy to choose and compose. Almost invariably, Lionel achieves an easy informality, born of his closeness to his subjects. What emerges, in the atmospheric colouring of the Autochrome, is a picture of the higher reaches of the Edwardian world, relaxed and smiling, always in sunshine. It is hard not to look at them and reflect on the upheaval which was to overturn their world within a few years.

Some 250 Autochromes were taken of English houses and gardens, by far the largest group of these in the gardens of Ascott, the family home designed for Lionel's father Leopold in the 1880s. Lionel never entered the house with his camera. The inordinate length of exposure required for the Autochrome and the ease with which colours could be upset by poor light or wrong exposure were enough of a deterrent for him. And anyway, his interests and pleasure lay outside in the gardens, whether in the formality of the topiary gardens or the opulent drifts of spring-flowering bulbs which Lionel's father Leopold had planted in the surrounding meadows, often providing Lionel with some of his richest capturings of colour, as tulips or daffodils sprang up and burst into seas of colour beneath blossoming trees.

Other images were taken at the older family home at Gunnersbury in west London, where a favourite time of year was the flowering of the lilies in the pond before the house. But the gardens of friends, both great and small, were also favoured. Among recognisable places is the Palladian Bridge at Stowe; more intimate in scale are the Essex gardens of the Du Cane family. Close-up studies of flowers, rural scenes of heath with gorse, the interiors of glasshouses: all were of interest to him. Occasional close-ups betray a plantsman's detailed fascination but the simple setting of flowers within a landscape was just as pleasing to Lionel's eye, as well as providing the ideal testing ground for composition and, above all, for the subtlety of contrast or complementarity of colour offered for the first time by the Autochrome.

Of the remainder, some four hundred in number, most were taken on Lionel's tours in Europe and North Africa. For him, as for so many of us, photography remained largely a holiday habit. As at home, so abroad, the theme of plants and trees in landscapes recurs often: in a corner of a Mediterranean garden, the sun on a terracotta pot draped by a curtain of cypresses or a tree heavy with oranges against a background of mountains and sea.

But there was also an educational strain to Lionel's work. Whether in Egypt, Rome or Pompeii, his eye was drawn, like any other tourist, to the ruins of past civilisations, but his was an eye tempered by a clear interest in the detail of those long-gone societies. We know from his surviving lecture notes that he prepared at least two sequences of plates to be projected for an audience, one on classical Italy based on his 1912 honeymoon tour, the other on ancient Egypt. The notes betray wide reading in and around his subjects to bring to life the world whose magnificent vestiges he was capturing in his lens.

And then there are the less easily categorised images, smaller in number and shot, almost certainly, to explore the new medium. A few are still-life compositions, of flowers in a vase with oranges and books, or maize-cobs laid out to dry on a sun-baked stone wall. They seem to echo the elegant compositions of the Photo-Secessionists whose work Lionel would have seen in the early exhibitions of Autochromes in London. There are attempts (many of them brave but unsuccessful) to challenge the technical difficulty of capturing broad sunset skies at dusk. And there is the fascinating handful of images of animals and birds, perhaps the earliest surviving images in colour of the Zoological Gardens in London. There is no better proof of Lionel's ability to transcend the range of the average photographer than his picture of the tiger, languidly stretched out in the foreground, indifferent to the curious and restless stares of the seemingly caged crowd, viewed through the bars in the background.

Victor Gray is the former Director of The Rothschild Archive

A selection of Lionel de Rothschild's photographic equipment, including his half-plate field camera made by Ross, London, a spare lens, darkslides, exposure meters and exposed Autochrome plates. *(Photograph by David Giles)*

LIONEL DE ROTHSCHILD'S AUTOCHROMES

1   KING EDWARD VII,
    STRATHSPEY, SEPTEMBER 1909

Perhaps Lionel's greatest photographic coup
was this informal portrait of King Edward VII
in Highland costume, taken in September 1909
on one of Lionel's regular excursions to Scotland
for the autumn grouse season somewhere near
the Sassoon family's hunting lodge at Tulchan in
Strathspey, just fifteen miles from Balmoral.
Eight months later, Edward was dead. To date,
no earlier colour photograph of Edward has
been identified.

MARIE DE ROTHSCHILD
AT GUNNERSBURY, *c.*1910

A relaxed informal portrait of Lionel's mother, seated on the terrace at Gunnersbury with her much coddled pet Maltese terrier. Marie de Rothschild (1862–1937), the daughter of Achille Perugia, an Austrian banker from Trieste, had married Leopold in 1881 in the presence of Prince Edward, the first occasion on which the future king had attended a Jewish marriage ceremony. Her sister, Louise, was married to Arthur Sassoon and visits to the Sassoon hunting lodge in Scotland were a regular part of the family's calendar.

LEOPOLD DE ROTHSCHILD BESIDE HIS
LILY POND AT GUNNERSBURY, *c.*1910

Lionel's father, Leopold (1845–1917) was one of three brothers who together ran the family bank from the late 1870s, following the death of their father. Outside the bank, Leo was heavily involved with horse racing, breeding horses at his Southcourt Stud and producing a number of notable winners. He was also a keen gardener (a passion which he handed on to his son), developing the garden at Gunnersbury in west London, inherited from his father, and laying out a new garden at his house at Ascott in Buckinghamshire.

NO.5

4   LIONEL'S BROTHER, EVELYN
DE ROTHSCHILD AT ASCOTT, 1912

The middle of three brothers, Evelyn was
four years younger than Lionel and in his mid-
twenties when this picture was taken at Ascott,
probably in 1912. Two years after the photograph
was taken Evelyn joined the Royal Bucks
Hussars. On the outbreak of war along with his
friend and cousin the Hon. Neil Primrose, M.P.
son of Lord Rosebery. They both died in action
in Palestine in November 1917.

5   LEOPOLD DE ROTHSCHILD
IN HUNTING PINK, c.1909

Lionel's father was a passionate huntsman
throughout his adult life, riding regularly with
the Rothschild Staghounds, first established by
his father in 1839. The kennels for the hunt
were housed at Ascott.

6   MARIE-LOUISE BEER,
LIONEL'S FIANCÉE, 1912

Lionel's future wife was the daughter of a
Parisian financier. They were engaged in
August 1912 and married in October. This
informal photograph was probably taken at
the time of the engagement. Her new ring is
clearly displayed, though she still wears black
following the recent death of her father.

NATHANIEL, 1ST LORD ROTHSCHILD AT ASCOTT, *c.*1910

Lionel's uncle Natty (1840–1915) was the mainstay of the family bank, N.M. Rothschild & Sons and one of the most powerful and respected financiers in Europe. He had been made a peer in 1885, the first Jewish peer ever to be created, and had been a friend of the King since their Cambridge days. In his late 60s when photographed here at Ascott, he was increasingly deaf and seen as something of an austere autocrat, but Lionel has managed to catch a softer edge in this portrait of his uncle.

8

ALFRED DE ROTHSCHILD AT GUNNERSBURY, *c.*1910

Lionel's other uncle, Alfred (1842–1918) was very different from his brother Natty. Although like him a partner in the family bank, he enriched his life with broader tastes, particularly for theatre (he was involved with the Gaiety Theatre) and art (he was a Trustee of the National Gallery and the Wallace Collection and a major collector in his own right). The house which he built at Halton, six miles from Ascott, was a lavish confection, filled with an over-rich collection of paintings and furniture. Alfred is seen here on the south terrace of the Large Mansion at Gunnersbury.

NO. 5

10 THE PRIME MINISTER, H.H. ASQUITH,
    *c.*1910

The Prime Minister, H.H. Asquith, caught in a
casual moment. Asquith was a frequent visitor to
Rothschild and Sassoon houses. His second wife,
Margot Tennant was a very close friend of Aline
Sassoon (*née* de Rothschild).

11   MILITARY ENCAMPMENT,
      TIDWORTH, WILTSHIRE, 1911

Lionel had been a 2nd Lieutenant with the
Royal Bucks Hussars since 1903 and took part in
annual training encampments with the regiment.
In 1911 he was with the Bucks Hussars alongside
other regiments in camp at Windmill Hill near
Tidworth Barracks in Wiltshire. This and other
images almost certainly date from that time.

(following page)

12   LADY HELEN VINCENT, c.1910

Lady Helen Vincent, wife of the diplomat
Sir Edgar Vincent, was one of the great Edwardian
beauties, painted by Sargent in 1904. In 1906
Lionel had driven her, together with Muriel
Wilson and Winston Churchill, across Italy at
a breakneck speed of 40 m.p.h.

NO.11

13

14

A FASHIONABLE GUEST AT ASCOTT, *c.*1910

Another of Lionel's portraits of guests at an
Ascott weekend house-party. The subject has
not been identified but the view is across the
Vale of Aylesbury and the costume worthy of
any Edwardian fashion plate.

THE HON. WILLIAM BROWNLOW PLAYING GOLF AT ASCOTT, *c.*1910

The young Hon. William Brownlow, in sailor
suit, practising his golf in the gardens of Ascott.
He later represented Britain in the Walker Cup
against the U.S.A. in 1926. This is one of only
two portraits by Lionel of children

NO.15

15   THE SOUTH FRONT OF ASCOTT HOUSE,
      BUCKINGHAMSHIRE, *c.*1909

A romantic image of the south front of Ascott,
the home of Lionel's parents. The house had
been much extended and altered in the 1880s
around the core of an original farmhouse to
designs by the architect George Devey, creating
an 'Old English' manor house. At the time
Lionel photographed it, the heavy mantle of
wisteria and roses was adding to the romantic
feel of the property. The precisely clipped
topiary was also a reflection of the Arts and
Crafts fashion of the period.

16   THE DUTCH GARDEN, ASCOTT, *c.*1909

Symmetrical beds, formal planting and bold
colour combine with whimsical topiary in the
Dutch Garden at Ascott. At the centre stands
the Cupid Fountain, by the sculptor Thomas
Waldo Story.

NO.17

17 Mound planting at Ascott, c.1909

The banking of soil around the trunk of a tree was a widely practised Victorian method of planting mature trees, reducing the need to dig deep into the soil and providing greater stability for the tree as it grew. Here, however, mounds seem to have been used to provide opportunities for highly visible massed bedding, producing striking spring colour.

18 The south-west corner of Ascott House, c.1909

The garden here displays two of Ascott's most characteristic features at the time: the widespread use of elaborate and monumental topiary and the raised beds of mound planting laden with colour. *Country Life*, describing Ascott's gardens in 1900, spoke of 'quaintly clipped yews cut into shapes that those who revile topiary work consider a form of shrub slaughter'.

19   TIGER AT LONDON ZOO, *c.*1910

One of the most atmospheric of Lionel's
photographs, shot through the bars of one of the
outside cages of the Lion House at London Zoo.
The tiger's languid indifference to the visitors who
stare with almost animal fascination, seemingly
from behind bars, creates a memorable image.

(following page)

20   KING PENGUIN WITH KEEPER,
LONDON ZOO, *c.*1910

The penguin has proved more patient than
his keeper in pausing for the long exposure
time required by the Autochrome.

NO.19

NO.20

24 AVENUE OF BAMBOOS IN A
JAPANESE GARDEN

Lionel seems to have been fascinated by
the contemporary fashion for Japanese
gardens, of which his father had created
a celebrated example at Gunnersbury.
Though we cannot be sure where he
found this example, his image, dappled
with light and splashed by the leaves of
the bamboo, captures the spirit of the
garden wonderfully.

25 DETAIL OF PAVILION IN THE
JAPANESE GARDEN, CHÂTEAU
DE BOULOGNE, FRANCE, c.1909

This Japanese Garden had been created at
Lionel's cousin Edmond's estate near Paris.
Lionel has produced a well structured
composition, combining his interest in
the Japanese style with his oft-repeated
delight in the juxtaposition of the textures
of statuary and foliage. Nowhere perhaps
among Lionel's Autochromes has he used
the softness of light and colour to such
good effect. The gardens at Boulogne
eventually fell into disuse and have now
disappeared.

27   THE TEMPLE AT GUNNERSBURY, *c.*1909

The Temple pre-dates the Rothschilds' acquisition
of Gunnersbury Mansion in 1835. Originally an
ornamental dairy, it was, in Lionel's day, a garden
retreat in front of the circular pond used for
boating and a home for the family's flamingos

NO.28

LILIES WITH GARDEN SEAT

The combination of garden statuary or furniture with foliage is a repeated theme in Lionel's garden pictures. Here the clean-cut lines of the garden seat stand out sharply against the less disciplined leaves of fern, topped by the star-like flowers.

A VASE OF ROSES

Rarely did Lionel's studies of flowers have a purely aesthetic rather than a horticultural interest but in this soft-focused study of a vase of roses Lionel comes closest to the Autochromes of the Photo-Secessionists, the group of American photographers who were attempting to restore to photography the qualities by which the older visual arts were judged.

NO. 29

O   THE AVENUE OF THE RAM-HEADED
     SPHINXES AT KARNAK, EGYPT, 1910

In the spring of 1910, Lionel set off in his
6-cylinder Napier for North Africa, crossing from
Marseille into Algeria and then travelling along the
coast. Egypt was a favourite new destination for
British society, though most took the easier option
of a tour arranged by Thomas Cook. At the great
temple complex at Karnak, Lionel used light and
shadow to give atmosphere to his Autochrome
of the Avenue of Ram-Headed Sphinxes.

following page)

I   THE TEMPLE AT ABU SIMBEL,
     EGYPT, 1910

One of the most popular but more remote
destinations was the Great Temple built by
Ramses II at Abu Simbel, visited by Lionel, who
photographed its façade with the huge carvings
of Ramses, 67 feet high.

33   MARIE-LOUISE DE ROTHSCHILD
   IN ROME, 1912

Following their marriage in October 1912, the
Rothschilds' honeymoon tour took them first to
Rome, where Lionel's frenzied photographing of
the classical buildings in which he was so keenly
interested was tempered by a number of studies
of his new wife posed among the remains.

34   ROME, THE ARCH OF TITUS
   AND THE COLOSSEUM, 1912

At the time of the Rothschilds' visit, the
area around the Arch of Titus was still being
excavated and visitors were kept back behind
the fence (right).

35   THE COLOSSEUM, ROME, 1912

36   ST. PETER'S SQUARE, ROME, 1912

      Two views by Lionel of Rome in the days
      before mass tourism.

NAPLES AND MOUNT VESUVIUS, 1912

Lionel and Marie-Louise's honeymoon trip
to Italy moved south from Rome to Naples.
Along the coast a number of friends, including
Lionel's relation, the former Prime Minister,
Lord Rosebery, had villas. This stereo view of
Naples from the west, with Vesuvius behind,
topped by cloud, formed part of the lantern-
lecture which Lionel prepared on his return.

39   VILLAGERS IN A STREET, ?ITALY, 1912

Because of the difficulties of persuading local people to pose for the long exposure times required for the Autochrome, Lionel rarely included figures in his photographs. This stereo study of a young girl and elderly man in a town street is an exception, possibly dating from Lionel's Italian tour of 1912.

(preceding pages)

40   MEDITERRANEAN GARDEN DETAIL,
      >1912

      Lionel was as much attracted by the features
      as by the sweep of gardens, lingering on details
      and corners that others might overlook but
      which caught his eye for the interest of their
      composition, texture and colour.

41   VILLA GARDEN, THE BAY OF NAPLES,
      1912

      One of a number of gardens visited by
      Lionel and Marie-Louise in 1912. Lionel's
      constant fascination with ruins and statuary
      in a landscape made this an almost inevitable
      scene to catch his attention.

42   MEDITERRANEAN HARBOUR,
      ITALY, 1912

      A timeless image of a small Mediterranean
      harbour, taken on Lionel's honeymoon trip
      to Italy in 1912. The location has not yet
      been identified.

NO. 42

NO.44

43

COUNTRY LANE WITH GORSE

Lionel's motoring excursions and trips to house parties took him to many parts of the country. This may well be the plate referred to in a surviving index of a few of his plates as 'English landscape in July, Worcestershire'.

44

SUNSET, NORFOLK BROADS, c.1910

Lionel's attempts to explore the limits of the Autochrome process led to a number of experiments with limited light, many of which failed. However, in this image which he entitled 'Sunset, Norfolk Broads' he achieved a brooding and reflective atmosphere without loss of colour quality.

WADDESDON MANOR: *the splendour recaptured*

SOPHIEKE PIEBENGA, VICTOR GRAY

A touch of mystery surrounds the clutch of ninety glass photographic plates which were brought one day in the 1960s to Waddesdon Manor, wrapped in tissue paper and nestling in a wicker basket. There is no question of their historical importance because, when held up to the light, they revealed the house and gardens – now much altered by time but seen here as originally created by Baron Ferdinand de Rothschild and his sister Alice. Here they were, displayed in the soft colour of the Autochrome and lifted into startling three-dimensional realism by the magic of stereoscopy.

Waddesdon Manor was built by Baron Ferdinand de Rothschild (1839–1898) during the 1870s and 1880s to designs by the French architect Gabriel-Hippolyte Destailleur. Perched on top of a hill overlooking the Buckinghamshire countryside, it reflects the style of a 16th-century French château. The surrounding park landscape was laid out by another Frenchman, the landscape gardener Elie Lainé, in a largely informal style. The ornamental pleasure grounds, however, were created during the 1880s, under the Baron's own direction, by his head gardener Arthur Bradshaw (and his successor John Jaques) and the estate manager George Sims.

In contrast to the house, the planting of the gardens was distinctly Victorian, with formal, bright floral schemes, using tens of thousands of annual bedding plants, and bold groupings

---

Miss Alice at the door of Waddesdon Manor.

of colourful shrubs. A large ornamental aviary, built in 1889, had its own garden setting. Further down the hill was a huge range of glasshouses displaying more tender plants (especially orchids), long enclosed borders with roses and herbaceous plants, and extensive fruit and vegetable gardens. Nearby was the water garden with rockwork designed by the firm of James Pulham, and a dairy surrounded by its own intimate garden.

In 1875, shortly after Baron Ferdinand had bought the Waddesdon estate, his younger sister, Alice de Rothschild (1847–1922), acquired the adjoining property of Eythrope. Here she built The Pavilion and laid out her own garden for entertaining and display, the three-dimensional bedding schemes being a special feature.

Alice inherited the Waddesdon estate after Ferdinand's death in 1898. Single, determined and authoritative, she was by all accounts a formidable lady. Keen on all aspects of gardening, she involved herself closely with the upkeep of the grounds. 'Quality is the one thing you must study in all your work at Waddesdon', she insisted to her head gardener, George Frederick Johnson.[1] She even had him grow her fruit and vegetables in specially imported soil from nearby Brill and from Market Harborough in Leicestershire, claiming that the best Waddesdon loam produced but an acid tasting fruit.

It was at this time, when Miss Alice wielded the sceptre at Waddesdon, that the Autochromes were taken, although exactly when and by whom is not clear. They seem unlikely to be the work of a local professional; they have no pretensions to great composition, nor are they technically perfect. It seems more likely that they were taken either by a guest who happened to be an enthusiastic photographer or (less likely, given that Miss Alice was herself a subject of one of the plates) by a senior member of the estate staff.

All ninety plates are stereoscopes, the twin images shot simultaneously using one of the many stereo cameras available and popular at the time. Some of the plates still bear the inscription 'Richard Verascope', a make of cameras, accessories and viewers manufactured by the French company of Jules Richard from the 1890s to the 1930s. The handsome little Verascope viewer accompanied the plates and still survives at Waddesdon. Of the ninety images, 26 have been photographed in monochrome, the rest in Autochrome colour. Sixteen show interiors of the house, five are of people (three gardeners, a chauffeur and Miss Alice herself), and the remainder feature the gardens of both Waddesdon and Eythrope.

The interiors are of details of rooms, many of them taken in Miss Alice's sitting room. We see walls densely hung with drawings and watercolours, Sèvres porcelain and sculpture on furniture and mantelpieces, part of Miss Alice's collection of arms and armour, as well as some of Ferdinand's key acquisitions. Exactly why these particular views were chosen is not clear but they may have been taken for security purposes or as a matter of record to show where things were placed. These interiors demonstrate all the problems inherent in taking Autochromes within the house. Judging the length of exposure was always a difficult problem and the results here are variable. Nevertheless, it is clear that the photographer was taken with the challenges which interiors presented: no less than four of them are taken looking into a mirror.

Outside, in the gardens, the photographer is mainly interested in details: the corner of a floral bed, a display within a glasshouse, a path among shrubs. In these details, there is much which tells us about the original layout and style of the formal bedding which had been such a feature of the estate before the First World War.

During the war years, while estate staff left for the front, some of them never to return again, lawns were given over to sheep, potatoes and vegetables replaced flowers in the bedding schemes, the aviary was used for fattening rabbits and weeds were allowed to invade the drives. Even after the war, there was no urge for the surviving members of the garden staff to return to Waddesdon, as the Gardeners' Bothy was still being used to house German prisoners of war.

When, in December 1918, the head gardener at Eythrope, Gibbs, died, Miss Alice decided to scale down its gardens. Writing to Johnson, she suggested: 'In spring, if I am spared, we can go over Eythrope together and arrange the glass [houses] and gardens on a different footing – I shall not require it any longer as a show place.'[2]

Miss Alice's health had steadily deteriorated during the war and she died in 1922. The estate was left to her cousin James de Rothschild (1878–1957) and his young wife Dorothy (1895–1988). The economic climate of the 1920s demanded change and the glasshouse complex and kitchen garden at Waddesdon were given over to commercial enterprise. Of necessity the pleasure gardens were neglected and by the early 1930s the last of the flowerbeds had disappeared. After James' death in 1957, the Manor and its pleasure grounds were left to the National Trust who managed the property with much input from Mrs Dorothy de Rothschild. It was after her death in 1988, that her heir, Jacob, 4th Lord Rothschild (b.1936) initiated a large-scale restoration of the house and gardens.

It was during the restoration that the Waddesdon Autochromes came into their own, providing an invaluable source of information on the gardens as they were at the height of their Edwardian splendour and before the enforced changes of later years. With their aid, the bedding schemes on the terraces were faithfully reinstated. A few years later the aviary was fully restored and the long-lost original exuberant bedding layout which adjoined it was recreated. Today, the three-dimensional colours captured on the photographic plates almost a century ago have been brought back to life and the splendour of Waddesdon Manor and its gardens, now open to the public, can once again be experienced and enjoyed as Miss Alice knew them.

Sophieke Piebenga is Gardens Archivist for Waddesdon Manor

NOTES

1   Letter from Alice de Rothschild, 20 November 1906 (Johnson Letters, Waddesdon Manor: Acc. No. 84.1998).

2   Letter from Alice de Rothschild, 2 December 1918 (Johnson Letters, Waddesdon Manor: Acc. No. 84.1998).

Verascope stereoscopic viewers used to view the Waddesdon plates. *(Photograph by Mike Fear)*

THE WADDESDON AUTOCHROMES

45 WADDESDON MANOR
FROM THE NORTH, c.1910

Formal Victorian flowerbeds in close
juxtaposition with the façade of the 16th-
century French style of Ferdinand's house,
built between 1874 and 1889 to designs by
Gabriel-Hippolyte Destailleur.

46   BEDDING ON THE PARTERRE,
     c.1910

One of the principal features of the
garden was the extensive display of
Victorian bedding Mounded flower be
planted especially with pelargoniums a
begonias, were punctuated with 'dot
plants', such as New Zealand flax
(Phormium).

47   WADDESDON MANOR
     FROM THE PARTERRE, c.1910

Detailed images such as this, clearly
showing the types of plant used in the
Victorian bedding (pink pelargonium,
golden pyrethrum, blue lobelia) helped
to inform the reinstatement of the
bedding in the 1990s.

48   FORMAL BEDDING AT
     EYTHROPE, *c.*1910

At Eythrope, Alice de Rothschild's
original home adjoining the Waddesdon
estate, formal flowerbeds were as
significant a feature as at Waddesdon,
though on a smaller scale and of a more
intimate character.

49   TERRACE AND FOUNTAIN, *c.*1910

The centrepiece of the terrace is the
early 18th-century fountain of Pluto and
Proserpine, part of a fountain made by
Giuliano Mozani for the Farnese palace
at Colorno near Parma in northern Italy.

NO.50

50   GARDENER, WADDESDON MANOR, *c.*1910

One of the foremen working under G.F. Johnson, Waddesdon's head gardener for almost fifty years from 1905. It may well be Fred Sawyer, the 'heavily moustached' foreman of the main range of display glasshouses, collectively known as 'Top Glass'. This image was taken using the Verascope system with its distinctive rounded corners.

51   DISPLAY HOUSE, *c.*1910

A magnificent stand of campanulas amidst ferns in one of more than forty display glass houses built at Waddesdon by the firm of R. Halliday & Co.

NO.52

52   **THREE-DIMENSIONAL BEDDING
      AT EYTHROPE,** *c.*1910

A witty example of three-dimensional
bedding in the form of a flower basket.
The Rothschild gardeners excelled at
this type of sculptural bedding, the first
example of which was at Halton House,
home of Alfred de Rothschild.

53   **THE WATER AND ROCK GARDEN,**
      *c.*1910

The water and rock garden, constructed
by the firm of Pulham & Son in the 1880s,
using Pulham's celebrated artificial
rockwork. Overgrown and neglected, the
garden was recovered in the 1990s and
subsequently restored and replanted.

NO.54

54   BEDDING AT THE AVIARY, c.1910

Victorian flower beds in front of the
aviary, which had been built in 1889 in
time for the visit of the Shah of Persia.
Both bedding and aviary were later
neglected. The aviary was first restored
in the 1960s but it was not until 2003
that the original bedding scheme was
reinstated.

55   MISS ALICE'S SITTING ROOM,
WADDESDON MANOR, c.1910

Miss Alice's sitting room, hung with
red silk damask and heavily laden with
furniture and paintings. After her death
in 1922, the room was dismantled and its
contents distributed around the house.
The room is now the White Drawing
Room.